Happy Handwriting

Practice Book 4

Series Editor: Dr Jane Medwell
Author: Chris Whitney

William Collins' dream of knowledge for all began with the publication of his first book in 1819. A self-educated mill worker, he not only enriched millions of lives, but also founded a flourishing publishing house. Today, staying true to this spirit, Collins books are packed with inspiration, innovation and practical expertise.

They place you at the centre of a world of possibility and give you exactly what you need to explore it.

Collins. Freedom to teach.

Published by Collins
An imprint of HarperCollins*Publishers*
The News Building, 1 London Bridge Street, London, SE1 9GF, UK

HarperCollins*Publishers*
Macken House, 39/40 Mayor Street Upper, Dublin 1, DO1 C9W8, Ireland

> Browse the complete Collins catalogue at
> **collins.co.uk**

10 9 8 7 6 5 4 3

ISBN 978-0-00-848583-2

British Library Cataloguing-in-Publication Data
A catalogue record for this publication is available from the British Library.

Series editor: Dr Jane Medwell
Author: Chris Whitney
Expert Reviewer: Dr Mellissa Prunty
Publisher: Lizzie Catford
Product manager: Sarah Thomas
Project manager: Jayne Jarvis
Development editor: Jilly Hunt
Copyeditor: Jane Cotter
Proofreader: Oriel Square Ltd.
Cover designer: Sarah-Leigh Wills at Happydesigner
Design template and icons: Sarah-Leigh Wills at Happydesigner
Cover artwork: Jouve India Pvt. Ltd.
Illustrations: Jouve India Pvt. Ltd.
Typesetter: Jouve India Pvt. Ltd.
Production controller: Alhady Ali
Printed and bound in the UK using 100% renewable electricity at Martins the Printers Ltd.

Continue the pattern.

lluillull

Write over and copy.

if it ill tt ll ff ii al af

Sally shutter splat stall stuff

Write over and copy.

all tall bitter ruff staff fellow

Complete and copy the sentence below.

The clouds look flu __ __ y.

Are your ascenders the right height and parallel?

Continue the pattern.

pqf   pqf   pqf   pqf

Write over and copy.

pl   pr   gu   sp   fl   pl   pr   gu   sp   fl

happy   foggy   quill   jug

Write over and copy.

flower   primrose   daffodil

Complete and copy the sentences below into your book.

The _reen _elly wobbled on the plate.

Jiggling jelly is just delicious.

Are your descenders the right height and parallel?

Continue the pattern.

eeeeeeee

Write over and copy.

ei eigh ey el le ie ei eigh ey le ie

Write over and copy the rhyming pairs.

nettle kettle weight eight valley alley

Write over and copy.

vein obey let sleep week

Complete and copy the sentences below into your book.

The litt __ __ mackerel loves t __ __ sea.

It lives in a shoal and eats shrimps.

Remember! Joins to e are halfway up the letter.

Continue the pattern.

arenarenaren

Write over and copy.

er   re   un   ur   am   ai

aim   mine   jammy   pain   sew

Write over and copy.

Banana   ice   cream   is   nice

Copy the sentences below into your book.

A snail has no tail and carries its house on its back. It loves to eat leaves.

Are your short letters the same height?

Continue the pattern.

nmunmunm

Write over and copy.

mo   ng   mb   nn   mp

morning   climb   running   numb

Write over and copy.

environment   government   autumnal

Copy the haiku below into your book.

Autumn is coming

Orange leaves are falling down

Summertime has gone.

Making these letters the right height with the right spacing is the goal.

Continue the pattern.

ntlnltnlt

Write over and copy.

nt   ul   it   cl   id   ut

Anti- means against. Auto- means self or own.

Write over and copy.

automatic   anticlockwise

Write the words into your book in two lists: one for anti and one for auto.

antibacterial   autograph

autobiography   antiseptic

antisocial   autopilot

automate   antifreeze

Diagonal joins to tall letters join before the top of the tall letter.

✎ Continue the pattern, saying the name of the letter as you write.

lltlltlllt

✎ Write over and copy.

tt ee nn ss ll

letter sleep running class fall

✎ Write over and copy.

attic jetty splutter mattress committee

✎ Copy the sentences below into your book.

"The soil needs to be weed-free for seeds to grow," said Nell. "OK, let's get weeding!" Lee agreed.

Remember! Most double letters join but ss does not.

Continue the pattern quickly.

nypnyp

Write over and copy quickly.

jde krs der pt

Copy these words quickly.

dawdle   speedy   flash   along

Quickly copy the passage below into your book. Use a timer to check how long it takes.

After we have chewed and swallowed our food, it enters our stomachs. The stomach breaks down the food by mixing it around. The food is digested further in the intestine.

I can write 30 readable words in _____.

Continue the pattern.

No! No! No!

Write over and copy.

Wait! Stop! Come back!

Choose an exclamation from the ones above. Write it in a sentence using speech marks and exclamation marks.

said Ravi.

Add the exclamation marks and speech marks into the passage below, then copy into your book.

It was dark and there was a storm outside. Crash Bang Oh dear said Jack. What was that? A branch has fallen through the kitchen window said Mark. Oh no gasped Jack. There's glass everywhere

Do your speech marks show exactly what is said?

Add the punctuation marks to the sentence below. Then copy the complete sentence into your book.

Oh no said Edda the Viking One of our ships has sunk off the English coast

Assess your handwriting. Circle the face that shows how much you agree.

My joins between letters:

My letter height and spacing:

My double letters:

Copy the passage into your book.

Last week my class visited a museum. We saw fossils, including ammonites. My favourite part was examining dinosaur bones!

Assess your handwriting. Circle the face that shows how much you agree.

My letter e is joined:

The tails of my descenders are the right length:

I have not used joins after my b x y z s:

Look through your work this term. Copy and complete these targets into your book.

This term I have improved _____

I need to practise _____

Continue the pattern, saying the name of the letters as you write.

oeoeoeoeo

Write over and copy.

we ve fe oe

we were dove have poem toe safe

Write over the words.

shoe safe toes we wave were

fell goes went hive dove feast

Copy the sentences below into your book.

We went to see some live volcanoes last week. Lava spewed from the top. It was very exciting!

Can you keep the pen on the paper when making these joins?

Continue the pattern, saying the name of the letter as you write.

ererererer

Write over and copy.

ure rl are

Write over and copy the words.

measure treasure picture

nature pasture

Write over.

pleasure adventure girl burly hurl

Copy the sentence into your book.

"My treasured pearls and nature pictures have been stolen!" cried the elderly lady.

Check that you have kept r the right height.

Continue the pattern, saying the name of the letter as you write.

ouououou

Write over and copy.

ous   ious   eous

victorious   enormous   delicious

famous   spouse   outrageous

Add the missing word to the sentence and copy out into your book.

delicious   courageously   anxiously

The student waited _____.

That chocolate cake was _____.

The firefighters acted _____.

Can you keep the pen on the paper when making these joins?

Continue the pattern, saying the name of the letter as you write.

vlvlvl

Write over and copy.

fl wh ot

float flew what where when

spot trot joke poke out

Use these words to ask questions to a partner. Then copy the words onto the line below.

What? Why? When? Where?

Find the homophone pairs below and write each pair into your book.

flue flee floor flower flew flaw flour flea

Have you made your join go up as well as along?

Continue the pattern, saying the name of the letter as you write.

hahahahah

Write over and copy.

ha ed ing

as have had has having

Write over and copy the words below.

hedge medal half hand washed

Write the word *have has had* or *having* into these sentences, then copy them into your book.

_____ you _____ a good day today? Asma is _____ her dinner now. Jacques _____ been playing the piano this afternoon.

Have you noticed which letters do not join?

Continue the pattern, saying the name of the letter as you write.

bysbysbys

Write over and copy.

balloon yellow zoom buzz yes next

Write over and copy the sentence.

Today the weather is breezy with drizzle later.

Write over and copy the words into your book.

expect extinct exciting express expire

Find the pairs of rhyming words and copy them into your book.

next amaze spy moss sky
blaze blue boss you text

Check that s and z do not join at all.

Continue the pattern, saying the name of the letter as you write.

NRKNRKNRK

Write over the phrases and copy them into your book.

Priti's coat   Kim's lunchbox

David's pencil

Correct the passage, adding the capital letters and apostrophes. Then copy it into your book.

ms smiths ring was missing! she remembered wearing it on monday outside. she looked up at the magpies nest . . . could it be there? mr khan took a ladder and looked in the nest. "your rings here!" he shouted. "what naughty magpies!"

Remember! Capitals never join.

Continue the pattern, saying the name of the letter as you write.

ytlytlytl

Write over and copy the letter combinations.

y   ify   ily   y   ify   ily

Write over and copy the words.

rarity   speciality   terrify   community

Add the missing words and then copy out the sentence below into your book.

| *notify* | *qualify* | *immediately* | *family* |

The _____ had to _____
the school _____ if they were
to _____ for the reward.

Remember! You can join to y but not from it!

Continue the pattern, saying the name of the letter as you write.

lmnolmnolmno

Arrange these words in alphabetical order and write below.

| cherry |
| mango |
| plum |
| melon |
| apple |
| pineapple |
| apricot |

Add the missing letters and then copy out the alphabet into your book.

_ _ c d e _ _ _ i j k _ _ _ o p q r _ _ _ _ w x _ _

Write these words into your book in alphabetical order.

shouted   urged   pleaded   nagged

remarked   threatened   ordered

wailed   questioned

Do you know the alphabet by heart?

Add the missing words to the sentences.
Then copy the sentences into your book.

Have	had	asked	replied

"_____ you _____ your breakfast?"

_____ Mum. "I'm not hungry,"

_____ Rachel.

Assess your handwriting. Circle the face that shows how you feel about parts of your handwriting.

My horizontal joins from r are:

The space between y and other letters is:

My break letters (y, b, z, s, x) do not join to letters after them:

Copy the poem into your book.

Who? my friends and I

What? are going diving

Why? we're on our holidays!

Assess your handwriting. Circle the face that shows how you feel about parts of your handwriting.

My horizontal joins are:

The space between letters:

My apostrophes:

Look through your work this term. Copy these targets into your book and complete them.

This term I have improved _____

I need to practise _____

Copy all the letters of the alphabet
(without joining up) saying the name of the letter as you write.

a b c d e f g h i j k l m n o p q r s t u v w x y z

Print these words.

table chair computer pencil book

Draw a map of your classroom in your book. Write the labels below in print on your plan.
Use lines to connect the labels to the features on your plan.

whiteboard   table   chair
door   window

Draw a plan of the area around your school in your book. Write labels in print on your plan. Use
lines to connect the labels to the features on the plan.

entrance   road   playground

playing field   environmental area

classroom

Can you move from joined writing to print and back again?

Continue the repeating pattern.

369369

Copy the dates into your book.

Tuesday 3rd January

Friday 20th January

Wednesday 25th January

Copy the diary extract into your book.

Tuesday 3rd November

Today has been really exciting! We

have been building a bonfire ready

for Thursday's party. It will be the 5th

of November. Tomorrow, Wednesday,

we are going to the shops to buy the

food. I've invited 7 of my friends.

I can't wait.

Is your letter a always the same size?

Continue the pattern, saying the name of the letter as you write.

ouououou

Write over and copy the words.

young touch double trouble country

Add the missing words to the sentences and then copy out into your book.

| young trouble how touch |

A _____ goose is called a gosling.

"You'll get into _____ if you climb that wall," said Fallou.

"____ does this computer work?" asked Mohsin.

"It's _____-screen," said the teacher.

Check that the joins and spaces between letters are the same.

Continue the pattern.

caucaucau

Write over and copy.

ai   ch   wa   wh   ad

Copy the words quickly.

chip   want   where   add   then

Add the missing words to the sentences.

claimed	chips	where	add

Nobody _____ the umbrella.

_____ had it come from?

"_____ another portion of _____

to the order. I'm hungry!"

Now copy them out as quickly as possible into your book. Time yourself.

Are your letters the right height? Are the spaces even?

✎ Put the apostrophe in these phrases then copy them out.

The girls hats _____

The boys books _____

The babies toys _____

The childrens aunts _____

✎ Draw a circle around the plural words.

The cat's food

The passenger's glove

The cats' kittens

The girls' uniforms

The girl's friend

✎ Add an apostrophe to the words that need one. Then copy the sentences in your book.

The mens umbrellas were left in the corner.

The ladies cricket bats were in the pavilion.

The actresses wigs were in the dressing room.

Are your apostrophes clearly placed?

Continue the pattern.

dmi

Write over and copy the letter combinations.

dis   mis

Write over and copy the words.

disappoint   disagree   disobey

mislead   misbehave   mishear

Add dis- or mis- to these words to make them mean the opposite and copy them out.

_____ lead

_____ believe

_____ obey

_____ appear

_____ judge

_____ agree

Aim for correct spacing and correct height of letters.

✎ Continue the pattern, saying the name of the letter as you write.

BPTBPT

✎ Write over and copy the words.

Dhaka Santiago London India

Australia Yasawa Islands

✎ Add the capital letters and then copy the sentence into your book.

ali went to see his family in bolton on tuesday.

✎ Add the missing capital letters to this passage and copy it into your book.

nairobi is the capital city of the republic of kenya, in east africa. swahili is spoken there. kenya has coastline on the indian ocean. it is on the equator.

Remember to use a capital letter for a place or person.

Copy the numbers below.

1st 2nd 3rd 4th 5th 6th 7th 8th 9th

Copy the words below.

first second third fourth fifth

sixth seventh eighth ninth

Fill in the sentence with the word for each racer's position. Then copy out each complete sentence into your book.

1. Ed finished the race in ____ position.

2. Kai came ____.

3. Rav finished in ____ position.

Remember to use a hyphen when writing two-word numbers.

Complete the party-planning chart.

Who will I invite?	_____
What is the occasion?	_____
What time will it be?	_____
Where will it be?	_____

Complete the invitation below. Add:

- the name of the person you are inviting
- the date, place and time
- the date they must reply to you by
- your signature too.

Then copy it all out into your book using your best presentation skills.

Dear _____

I would like to invite you to my party! It will be held at _____ on _____ from _____ pm to _____ pm.

Please reply by _____

Yours sincerely,

_____

Check the presentation of your work, including the way any number names are written.

✎ Add the punctuation and capital letters, then copy the sentence into your book.

oh no said ms owen a fox has raided the hens house.

✎ Assess your handwriting. Circle the face that shows how you feel about each statement.

My apostrophe is spaced correctly:

My capital letters are correct:

My speech marks are clear and well-placed:

✎ Copy the passage into your book.

There are two types of common camels. The first type is called a dromedary. It has one hump. The second is called a Bactrian camel. It has two humps. They can both shut their nostrils during sandstorms.

✎ Assess your handwriting. Circle the face that shows how you feel about parts of your handwriting.

The height of my ascenders and descenders are:

My written numbers are:

I did not join b, x, y, z or s: